Crayola

LET'S DRAW ANIMALS WITH CRAYOLA!

ILLUSTRATED BY ANA BERMEJO

LERNER PUBLICATIONS ◆ MINNEAPOLIS

Official Licensed Product
Lerner Publications Company
A division of Lerner Publishing Group, Inc.
241 First Avenue North
Minneapolis, MN 55401 USA

For reading levels and more information,
look up this title at www.lernerbooks.com.

Main body text set in Billy Infant Regular 24/30.
Typeface provided by SparkyType.

Library of Congress Cataloging-in-Publication Data

Names: Bermejo, Ana, 1978– illustrator.
Title: Let's Draw Animals with Crayola! / illustrated by Ana Bermejo.
Description: Minneapolis : Lerner Publications, 2018. | Series: Let's Draw with Crayola! | Includes bibliographical references. | Audience: Ages 4–9. | Audience: K to Grade 3.
Identifiers: LCCN 2017009630 (print) | LCCN 2017018441 (ebook) | ISBN 9781512497762 (eb pdf) | ISBN 9781512432954 (lb : alk. paper)
Subjects: LCSH: Animals in art—Juvenile literature. | Drawing—Technique—Juvenile literature.
Classification: LCC NC780 (ebook) | LCC NC780 .D725 2018 (print) | DDC 743.6—dc23

LC record available at https://lccn.loc.gov/2017009630

Manufactured in the United States of America
1-41826-23786-7/31/2017

CONTENTS

CAN YOU DRAW ANIMALS?

You can if you can draw shapes! Follow the steps and use the shapes to draw colorful animals of the rain forest or fun animals on the farm. Or see if you can come up with a brand-new type of animal!

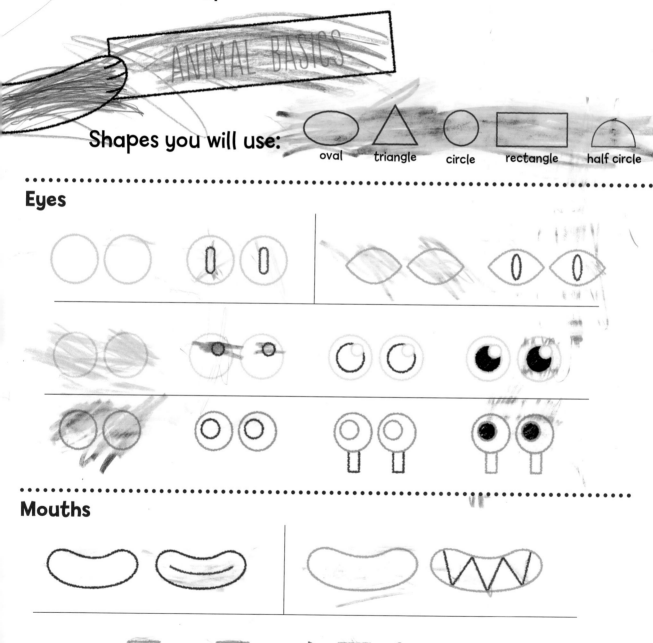

ANIMAL BASICS

Shapes you will use: oval triangle circle rectangle half circle

Eyes

Mouths

Paws and Feet

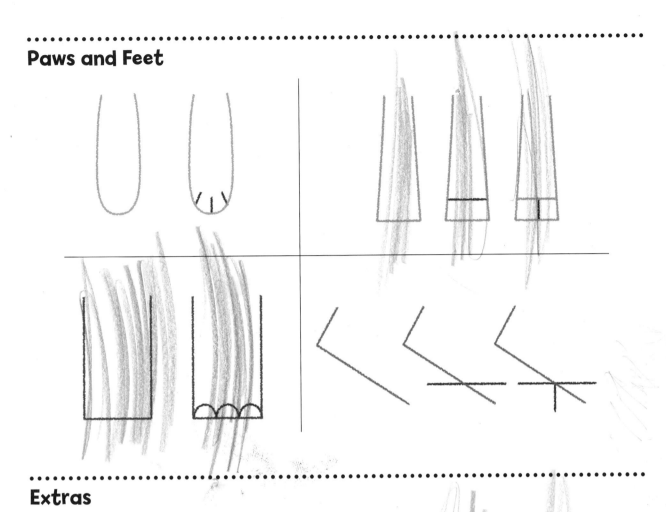

Extras

ears

wings

tails

Shapes you will use:

triangle   half circle   trapezoid   circle   oval

Rufus

Swishy

Prancy Fants

7

FARM ANIMALS

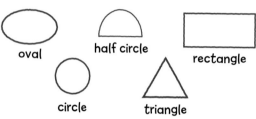
Piggy

Mother Hen

Billy

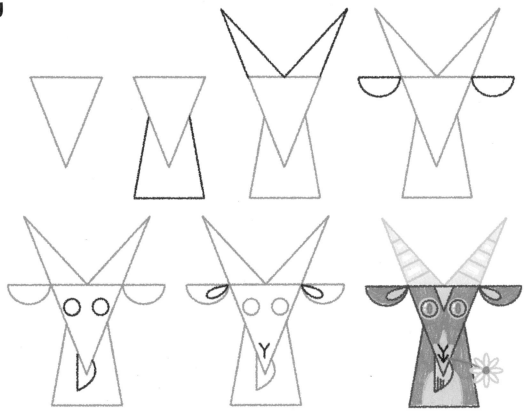

Chestnut

9

OCEAN ANIMALS

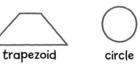

Annie Anemone

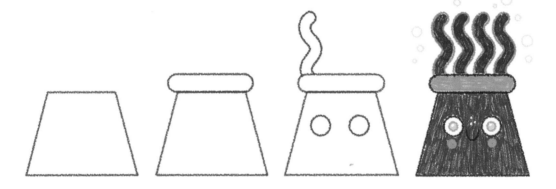

Otto

10

Chomp

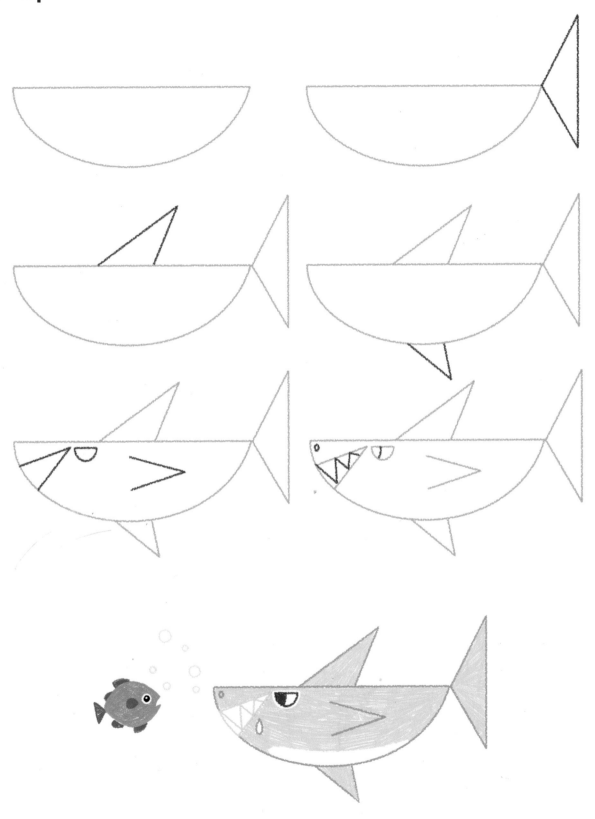

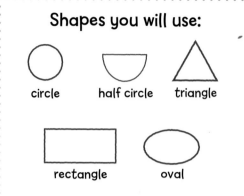

Shapes you will use:

circle   half circle   triangle

rectangle   oval

Mr. Monkey

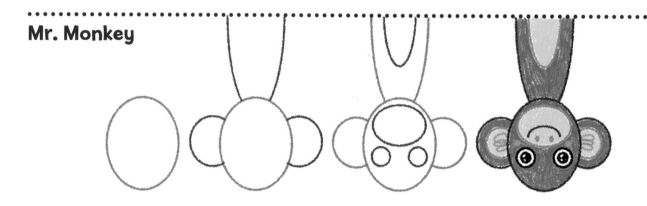

Sly Skater

Polly

Flutter

13

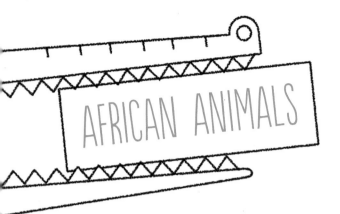

AFRICAN ANIMALS

Too Tall

Leo

Jumbo

15

POLAR ANIMALS

Shapes you will use:

 oval circle triangle half circle

Sealy

Paws

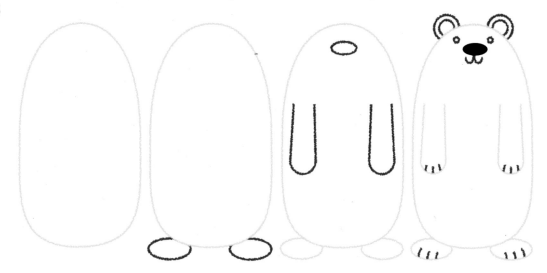

Tux

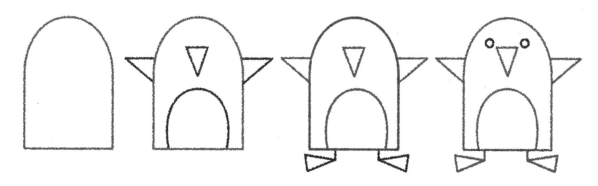

17

AUSTRALIAN ANIMALS

Shapes you will use:

 rectangle

 circle

 triangle

 oval

Emma Emu

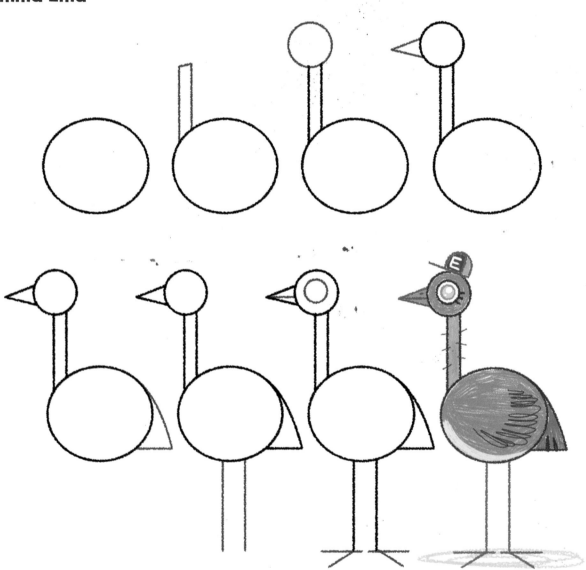

Klingin' Koala

Al E. Gator

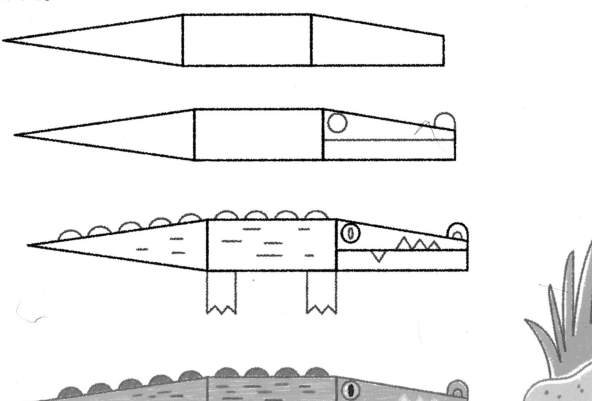

CRITTERS

Lady

Snappy

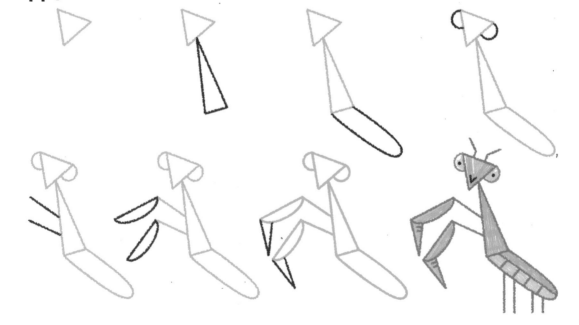

Webster

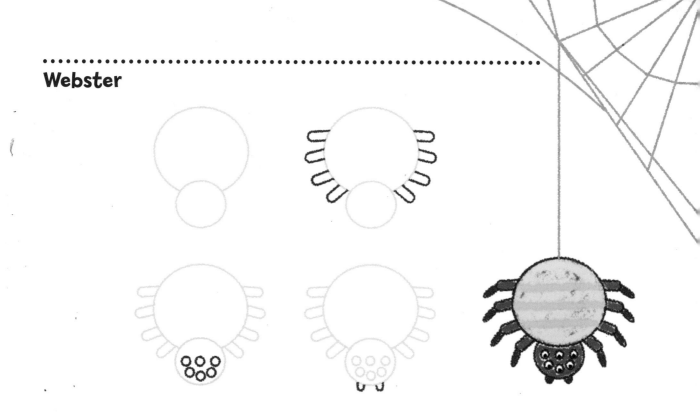

Squeak

Shapes you will use:

half circle

circle

triangle

trapezoid

Early Bird

Tweeter

22

Hootigan

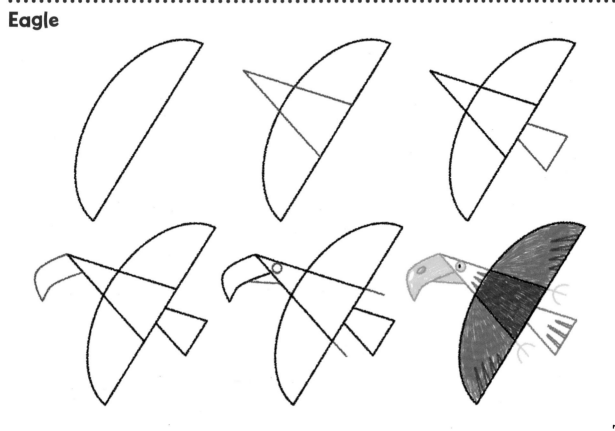

Eagle

23

GOOFY ANIMALS

Shapes you will use:

 circle   triangle   oval   half circle

Patty

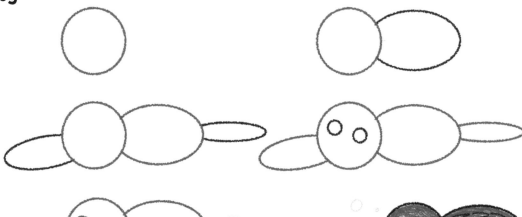

Blobby Blob Fish

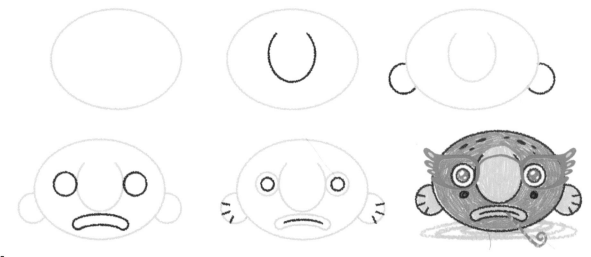

24

Kiwi Cutie

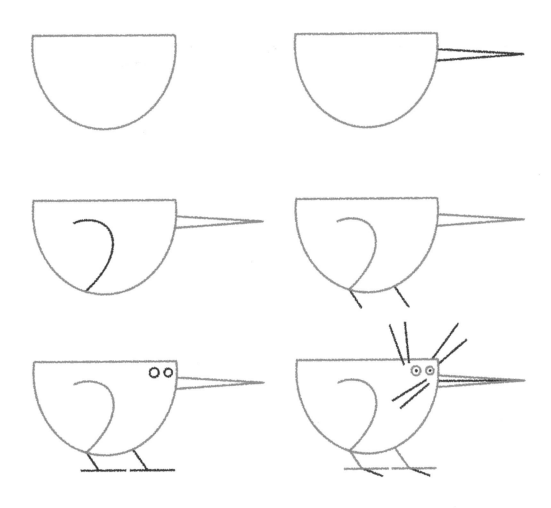

Not that kind of kiwi!

IMAGINARY ANIMALS

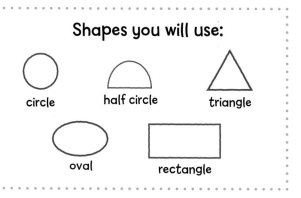

Shapes you will use:

circle | half circle | triangle

oval | rectangle

Catasaurus

Pigfish

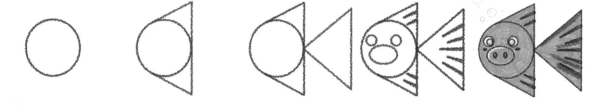

26

Flying Dogseal

Big-Eared Owlphant

ANIMAL PICNIC

28

WORLD OF COLORS

Colors are everywhere! Here are some of the Crayola® crayon colors used in this book. What kinds of colorful animals will you draw next?

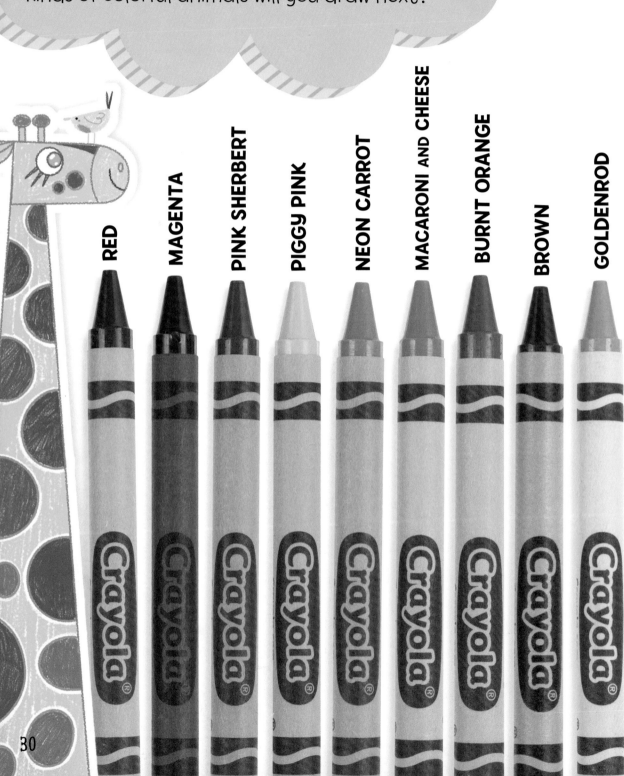

RED

MAGENTA

PINK SHERBERT

PIGGY PINK

NEON CARROT

MACARONI AND CHEESE

BURNT ORANGE

BROWN

GOLDENROD

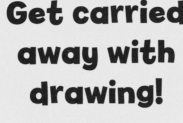

Get carried away with drawing!

YELLOW

INCHWORM

GREEN

SKY BLUE

TURQUOISE BLUE

WISTERIA

ROYAL PURPLE

GRAY

TIMBERWOLF

BLACK

Crayola®
Crayola®
Crayola®
Crayola®
Crayola®
Crayola®
Crayola®
Crayola®
Crayola®
Crayola®

31

TO LEARN MORE

Books

Bergin, Mark. *It's Fun to Draw Pets.* New York: Sky Pony, 2014.
Get more practice drawing your favorite pets with these
step-by-step instructions.

Brecke, Nicole. *Sea Creatures You Can Draw.* Minneapolis: Millbrook Press, 2011.
Check out this book to draw more animals from under the sea.

Legendre, Phillippe. *Animals around the World.* Irvine, CA: Walter Foster, 2015.
Take a look at this book to learn how to draw more animals from around
the world.

Websites

How to Draw Easy Animals
http://www.hellokids.com/r_575/drawing-for-kids/drawing-lessons
-for-kids/how-to-draw-animals/how-to-draw-easy-animals
Visit this website to get more practice drawing your
favorite animals from simple shapes.

MacDonald's Farm
http://www.crayola.com/crafts/macdonalds-farm
-craft/
Create your own farm by making a barn out of
cardboard materials and drawing your favorite farm animals.